WHEN HORSES PULLED BOATS
A *Story of Early Canals*

by
Alvin F. Harlow

Introduction by
William H. Shank, P.E.

Illustrated by
Orson Lowell
and
Philip J. Hoffmann

Published by
AMERICAN CANAL AND TRANSPORTATION CENTER
809 Rathton Road, York, PA 17403

First Printing — April 1983
Second Printing — August 1987
Third Printing — April 1994

ISBN 0-933788-43-6   Copyright William H. Shank, 1983

The Lock-Keeper's House

TABLE OF CONTENTS

Alvin Fay Harlow (1875-1963) 4

Introduction 5

Chapter I, Why Men Built Canals 7

Chapter II, One Hundred Years Ago 12

Chapter III, How Early Canals Were Built 16

Chapter IV, Some Early Canals 21

Chapter V, What Are Canal Boats Like? 25

Chapter VI, The Locks 28

Chapter VII, The Canal and the Farmers 35

Chapter VIII, What the Boats Carried 38

Chapter IX, How the Canals Helped Business 42

Chapter X, Wise Mules 44

Chapter XI, Low Bridge 47

Chapter XII, Life on the Canal 51

Chapter XIII, The Passenger Boats 55

Chapter XIV, Before Pullman's Day 58

Chapter XV, Line Boats and House Boats 61

Chapter XVI, What Have the Canals Done For Us? 64

Canal Bibliography 69

Other ACTC Publications 71

ALVIN FAY HARLOW (1875-1963)

Alvin Harlow was born March 10, 1875 in Sedalia, Missouri. His parents were John Edwin Harlow and Ann Elizabeth (Hawkins) Harlow. He was graduated from Franklin College in Indiana in 1899 with a Bachelor of Philosophy degree. Later (1929) he acquired a Doctor of Letters degree. He married Dora Shockley, June 10, 1909.

From 1908 to 1913 he was Secretary, Treasurer and Director of the Grand View Coal and Timber Corporation of Tennessee. He then spent nearly a decade as an advertising specialist and business-magazine writer. His work during this period included the production of an educational motion picture illustrating life in the Southern Appalachian Mountains. He produced his first major book: "Old Towpaths, The Story of the American Canal Era" in 1926.

During the ensuing twenty-five years he produced a steady stream of historical and fictional books, including such titles as: "Clowning Through Life" (with Edwin Foy); "Old Post Bags"; "Murders Not Quite Solved"; "Paper Chase"; "Old Bowery Days"; "Schoolmaster of Yesterday" (with Millard F. Kennedy); "Weep No More My Lady"; "Bret Hart of the Old West"; "Theodore Roosevelt-- Strenuous American"; "Steelways of New England"; "The Serene Cincinnatians"; "The Ringlings"; and "Young Telegraphers of the Civil War".

Harlow was a regular contributor to such magazines as Saturday Evening Post, American Mercury, Century, Collier's, and New Yorker. He also wrote various sections of the Book of Knowledge, the Book of Science, the Atlas of American History, and numerous encyclopedias. He died in New York City, November 17th, 1963 — a highly honored member of a number of author's leagues and historical organizations.

INTRODUCTION

Most canal historians in the United States are familiar with Alvin F. Harlow's classic work of 1926 entitled "Old Towpaths". Living in the declining years of the Nineteenth Century Canal Era, and becoming personally fascinated by it, Harlow's first major literary work covered the American Canals, over a hundred-year period, with exceptional realism and clarity. This fine work, with its more than 400 pages of carefully-researched technical information, colorful anecdotes and full-page illustrations, has become the "Bible" of canal buffs throughout the country.

Few of us were aware, however, that Harlow had also published an abbreviated version of "Old Towpaths" as a grammar-school textbook in 1936. This small book was evidently considered too unimportant to be mentioned by his biographers, or even by Harlow himself. It was not until a long-time friend of ours, Romaine Wills, showed it to us that we became aware of the existence of "When Horses Pulled Boats" by Alvin F. Harlow. Romaine told us she had found this book some years ago when she taught at the old Madison Elementary School in York.

Approaching the Lock

Ruth and I both sat down and read the book immediately. We were delighted with its simplicity and its clear-cut explanation of many badly neglected facets of the canal era. It was like suddenly opening a long-closed door on the past! We decided at once that we should make this little book available to historians, young and old, throughout the country. With the permission of Romaine Wills and the cooperation of the original publishers, we have done so!

There were blank spaces in the original book which we have used to inject additional illustrations. We have included all of the original sketches by Harlow's artist — Orson Lowell — but have added a number of more recent sketches by the late Philip J. Hoffmann, engineer-artist of Johnstown, Pennsylvania. Phil was perhaps the most authentic and prolific canal illustrator of the Twentieth Century. I have used many of his drawings in my own canal books, and also in "Canal Currents", house-organ of the Pennsylvania Canal Society. Phil frequently sent me small sketches, on old scraps of paper, to show details which he had uncovered in his personal canal research. I have carefully saved all of his drawings for an occasion such as this. Some of them are being reproduced in this book for the first time.

Hoffmann's illustrations tie in beautifully with Harlow's excellent text, and while different in style from Lowell's, have all the whimsy and charm of a child's fairy-tale! For good measure, I have added a few additional sketches from the original printing of my own "Amazing Pennsylvania Canals".

Therefore, we invite all historians — young and old — to travel backwards, through the pages of this book, to visit a world where life moved at a much more leisurely pace and was far less complicated than that of the "push-button" age in which we find ourselves.

York, Pennsylvania   William H. Shank, P.E.
April 1994   American Canal & Transportation Center

A Dutch Canal

Chapter I

WHY MEN BUILT CANALS

CENTURIES ago, so long ago that none of us can tell when it came about, primitive men first learned that they could make boats. We don't know how or when they first learned this, for no history has been written of those early times. No one then knew how to write; in fact writing had not even been thought of.

We now suppose that those early savage men must

have sat or stood on logs floating in the water, and that finally one of them said to his comrades, "Why not bind one or two of these logs together with vines? Then we will have a thing on which several of us can ride at the same time. Then we can cross this stream whenever we like."

And thus the first raft was made.

Later—it must have been centuries later—as their skill improved, the people learned how to make boats. Some of the earliest boats were just a light wooden frame-work, covered with the skins of animals, and were nearly round in shape.

As time went on and people began trading and selling things to other people who lived at a distance, they began to haul goods in their boats. This growing trade made it necessary not only to make a boat in which a man could ride, but one large enough for him to carry freight in, too. Soon men saw that you could easily carry more in a boat than on a horse's back.

Sometimes there was no river or lake on which to travel when men wanted to go across country from one river to another. Some of the rivers, too, were shallow, and some of them full of rocks and rapids. For this reason men began to dig canals.

Canals are artificial rivers. Some of the first ones were dug in very dry countries, such as Egypt, Assyria and Babylonia, so long ago that the dates are uncertain. We do know that ten thousand years ago there were canals in Egypt. The first canals, we think, were

WHY MEN BUILT CANALS

irrigation ditches—channels through which water was brought to some dry farming region to water crops.

It was not long before men began to put little canoes and dugouts into these canals. Presently the wiser men of the country said "Why not make the canals larger? Then we can place larger boats on them, and haul ourselves and our friends and our goods on them wherever we wish."

Then they discovered that these canals might be dug straight across where there were no rivers, or where the rivers were shallow and rough. As canals began to be built, they were used for travelling and for commerce. Ancient Babylon had several of them extending from the city to other important towns. One of these canals was seven hundred miles long. The Roman empire, which existed one thousand nine hundred years ago, built canals in Italy.

The Suez Canal cut through the Isthmus of Suez, which is the little neck of land connecting Africa and Asia, makes a water-way between the Mediterranean

An American Canal

On a Chinese Canal

and the Red Sea. Ships travelling between England and India, China or Australia, now go through the Suez Canal, instead of having to go all the way around the big continent of Africa, as they once did.

We think of the Suez Canal as a modern work, because it was opened in 1869. But think of it—there was a canal across that isthmus three thousand years ago! People have always known that it would be convenient to have a channel between those two seas. A canal was completed across the Isthmus of Suez one thousand three hundred and eighty years before the birth of Christ. It remained open and in use for one thousand five hundred years, and then it was neglected and its channel became filled up.

Canals were easy to dig in the low, flat countries like Holland and Belgium, and some were built there while the Romans still ruled those countries. To this day, a large part of Holland's commerce is carried on through its canals. Some of the most interesting sights in Holland are to be seen where patient horses plod along beside these waterways, pulling all sorts of boats, big and little.

In the Middle Ages a great many canals were built in Belgium, Holland, France, Germany, and other countries of Europe. Some of them are in use yet, though they are hundreds of years old. In China a great canal a thousand miles long was dug five hundred years ago. If you ever go to China, you will probably see it and its many queer-looking boats.

A German Canal

Chapter II

ONE HUNDRED YEARS AGO

BEFORE the United States became an independent nation in 1776, and for at least fifty years after that, there were no good roads in this country, and traveling was a dreadful task. There were no railroads until

ONE HUNDRED YEARS AGO 13

after 1830, and everybody had to ride about on horseback, or in carriages, wagons or stage-coaches drawn by horses. These vehicles would get stuck in the mud, time and again, and the travellers would have to get out and get their clothes and shoes dreadfully muddy. If two or three more horses could be found in the neighborhood, they would be borrowed and hitched on, to help pull the coach out of the mud. Sometimes this couldn't be done—the accident happened away out in the wilderness, where there were no houses, and no horses could be borrowed. Sometimes the travellers had to get out and walk, or wait until another carriage or wagon came along.

It was even harder to carry goods anywhere. Wagons were used wherever the roads were good enough. But some of the roads were poor and rough, and loaded wagons could not be taken over them. In many regions where very few people lived, there were no roads at all, only narrow trails through the forest. On these roads and trails, merchandise was carried on the backs of mules. Long caravans of mules, often a hundred or more in one train, were seen trudging through the forests and over the mountains with all sorts of goods tied on their backs.

Even before the United States became an independent nation, there were men who said that canals ought to be built. They knew about the canals in Europe. Some of them had traveled in Europe and had seen the canals there. They knew that two horses could draw a boat

14 WHEN HORSES PULLED BOATS

through still water loaded with a hundred tons of coal or stone or other things. Even on a good, level road, the same two horses could pull no more than one or two tons in a wagon, and if the road went uphill, they could not pull that much.

So people were thinking and talking about building canals. With canals they might travel and ship goods more easily and at less expense. They began planning routes for some of them. One was intended to connect Delaware Bay with Chesapeake Bay, so that a quick trip could be made between Philadelphia and Baltimore. Another was to be cut across the Cape Cod peninsula, in Massachusetts, so that boats passing between New York and Boston would not have to go around Cape Cod, which was a long and often very stormy journey. Another idea was to dig a canal from Lake Michigan, at the place where Chicago is now, down to the Illinois River, which runs into the Mississippi, and thus make a passage for boats between the Great Lakes and the Gulf of Mexico.

All three of these canals were built many years afterward, and are in use today.

George Washington, when he was a young man, believed that the Potomac and the James Rivers ought to be connected with the Ohio River by canal, so that commerce could be carried on between the people along the Atlantic coast and the pioneers who were beginning to settle in the Ohio Valley. To carry out his ideas, two canals were begun several years later,

ONE HUNDRED YEARS AGO 15

but the builders did not have money enough to complete them.

Many years passed before any of the canals which were planned could be built. The United States was a new nation, and very poor. Taxes were low, and neither the state governments nor the national government had much money to spend on public works, such as roads and canals. We had no millionaires; in fact, we had very few men whose fortune amounted to as much as a hundred thousand dollars. Therefore, it was hard to find anybody who had money to invest in building these things.

When the Middlesex Canal, connecting the city of Boston with the Merrimac River, was finally completed in 1803, it had cost more than $500,000; and that was such a great sum that the men who invested their money in it could never make any profit. To any of our big companies today, or to our government, a half a million dollars does not seem a large amount.

A Canal Aqueduct

Chapter III

HOW EARLY CANALS WERE BUILT

TRY to imagine how much harder it was to build canals a century ago than it is today. When you see a great steam shovel lifting huge masses of earth, heaping up a truck-load with only three or four shovelfuls, remember that the men who built our early canals had no such machines. Steam shovels had not been invented. Instead, hundreds of men with picks dug and loosened the soil, while other men with hand shovels threw it into wagons and teams of horses drew the wagons away to the place where the earth was dumped.

When they had to cut a canal channel through solid rock they had no dynamite with which to blast it out. They had only ordinary gunpowder, much less powerful than dynamite. Most of us have seen men drilling holes in rock into which dynamite is later put for blasting. Nowadays, they do this with machine drills. A man simply holds the machine drill upright on the rock, while it makes a loud clatter—"B-r-r-r-r-r-r-r-r-r-r-r-r!" and clouds of finely powdered rock dust fly up from it as the sharp, steel edge of the drill strikes the rock hundreds of times a minute, rapidly wearing the hole deeper and deeper.

HOW EARLY CANALS WERE BUILT 17

But a hundred years ago—even fifty years ago—when it was necessary to drill a hole in a rock, the workman took a long, heavy iron or steel bar, with its end sharpened to an edge, and lifted it and let it drop in the same spot. Each stroke of the drill on the rock broke loose tiny particles, thus slowly wearing a hole. It took two days to drill a hole which a modern machine drill can do in an hour or less.

When the hole was drilled, those early canal builders would pour it nearly full of gunpowder. Then they would put the end of a long fuse into the powder, and plug the mouth of the hole nearly full of soft clay. A man would light the fuse, and the workmen would hurry to a safe distance, just as you do after you light the fuse of a big fire-cracker on the Fourth of July. Then "Bang!" and off would go a mass of rock.

Nowadays we run a wire into the hole full of dynamite, and explode it by electricity. The dynamite breaks off a great deal more rock than the gunpowder used to do.

Just think of the famous *Deep Cut*, on the Chesapeake and Delaware Canal, which connects the lower end of the Delaware Bay with the upper part of Chesapeake Bay. This cut, more than a mile long, was mostly through solid rock, and ninety feet deep at its deepest point. At the time it was made it was one of the greatest works of the kind in the world. At one time, twenty-five hundred men were at work on it. Even with that army of men, it took five years of patient drilling and blasting to finish the job. It was worth all it cost; for by going through that little canal, only twenty-one miles long, boats saved themselves a five hundred mile journey through those two big bays, around Cape Charles and into the Atlantic Ocean, where they were in danger of storms and shipwreck.

How were these canals kept filled with water? The engineers who planned them arranged to take water from the rivers, creeks and lakes along the course. For this purpose a channel called a *feeder* was dug from lakes or streams near the canal, and strong, heavy gates were placed in this channel so that the quantity of water which ran into the canal through it could be controlled.

For some canals the water had to be brought a long way. The Delaware and Raritan Canal, for example, ran across the state of New Jersey from the Delaware River at Bordentown, up through Trenton, and then across to the Raritan River at New Brunswick. From New Brunswick the boats passed into New York bay. This canal therefore was a water-way between New York and Philadelphia. Most of the water for the canal came from the Delaware River, far above Trenton, through a feeder twenty-two miles long. The feeder was nearly as large as the main canal.

Every now and then the builders of a canal would come to a river or creek which ran right across its

HOW EARLY CANALS WERE BUILT

course, and they would have to build an aqueduct on which to cross. Built of stone or wood, and placed on piers much like the piers of a bridge, the aqueduct was simply a watertight trough through which the waters of the canal flowed across the stream. There was a foot-bridge or path beside it on which the horses or mules could cross, just as they would on an ordinary bridge.

The aqueduct had to be very carefully made to keep the water from leaking out. This gave the canal builders much trouble. We had no cement in America when the first canals were built. Cement was being made in Europe, but it cost so much to bring it across the ocean that the canal builders could not afford it.

About 1820, while the Erie Canal was being built, cement rock was discovered near it, between the cities of Utica and Syracuse. A factory was set up there, and cement was made and used on canal works after that. A little later, while other canals were being built, the same kind of rock was found near the Hudson, the Lehigh, and the Potomac Rivers. There are big cement factories in those very places today.

The first tunnels ever dug in the United States were made for canals. They were short cuts through hills, made to save the canal from going a long, long way around the hill. The very first tunnel built in this country was on the Schuylkill Canal, which ran along the side of the Schuylkill River, from Philadelphia up to Pottsville, in Pennsylvania. This tunnel was completed in 1821.

At that time there were as yet no railroads, and many people in America did not know what a tunnel was. A man wrote a letter to a newspaper, asking what was meant by a "tunnel." The editor of the paper did not know. He printed the man's letter in his paper, and under it he said, "Perhaps some other reader can tell us."

The second tunnel dug in America was near Lebanon, Pennsylvania. The Union Canal, which ran from the Schuylkill River to the Susquehanna River, passed through it. There were two other canal tunnels, one on the Chesapeake and Ohio Canal in Maryland being the longest—nearly a mile in length.

When a boat was going through a tunnel, it carried a lighted headlight and the men on the boat carried lanterns, just as if it were night.

A Canal Tunnel

Chapter IV
SOME EARLY CANALS

SOME of the first canals were short ones, dug around a waterfall or a rapid. They formed a sort of detour by which boats going up or down the river could pass out of the stream and around the rough places in smooth water. This done, the canal would bring them back into the river again.

Then longer canals were built. One ran from the Santee River to Charleston, in South Carolina. It was built so that boats coming down the river with grain, fruits and vegetables would not have to go out into the sea to reach Charleston, which was their best market.

The Middlesex Canal in Massachusetts was used in the same way. When people in New Hampshire wished to send their lumber, granite and farm products to Boston, they had to go down the Merrimac River and out into the ocean to reach the city. Otherwise they must unload the freight just before it reached the ocean and haul it twenty-five miles to Boston by wagon. After the Middlesex Canal was built, boats coming down the Merrimac just turned into the canal at Lowell and went straight on to Boston.

22   WHEN HORSES PULLED BOATS

Then still greater and longer canals were planned. The Erie Canal, although it was not quite the longest, was the busiest and most profitable of them all. It ran from Lake Erie at Buffalo to the Hudson River near Albany. Boats starting from Lake Erie could go all the way down to New York by the Hudson River. This canal was three hundred and sixty-four miles long. Work on it was begun in 1817, and it was completed in 1825. When we remember that it was all done without the help of the great machinery which modern builders have for digging and moving earth and rock, we must admit that to build the Erie Canal in eight years was doing very well.

The State of New York built several branches to the Erie Canal. One of these ran from the Hudson River to Lake Champlain. On it boats might go from New York City right up to Canada. Another branch ran from Syracuse to Oswego, on Lake Ontario. Other branches ran out into parts of the state which did not have any good way of sending their products to the cities.

The State of Pennsylvania also built a great system of canals. Its principal route crossed the state from Philadelphia to Pittsburgh, and there were several branches running out from it.

Many of Pennsylvania's most important canals were built to carry anthracite or hard coal. This coal was discovered in northeastern Pennsylvania about the year 1800. That small region is the only place in America

SOME EARLY CANALS 23

A Small Pennsylvania Coal Mine

where this kind of coal is found. When it was first discovered, there were no towns in that mountainous country; it was nearly all a wilderness.

At first, people did not believe that the hard coal would burn; they called it stone coal. When they had learned how to use it, it became very popular, and several canals were built for the purpose of carrying it to the cities. One of these, the Delaware and Hudson Canal, ran from Honesdale in Pennsylvania to the Hudson River. Through this canal, New York City first received its anthracite coal.

24 WHEN HORSES PULLED BOATS

Several other canals were built out from the hard coal region. One ran alongside the Schuylkill River, down to Philadelphia. Another followed the banks of the Lehigh and Delaware Rivers to Philadelphia. Another ran from Elmira, New York, along the banks of the Susquehanna River, all the way to Chesapeake Bay. Two canals were built across New Jersey, from the Delaware River to New York harbor. These two helped to bring New York's supply of anthracite coal from Pennsylvania.

A great many canals, like the ones we are talking about, ran close beside the banks of rivers. It was easier to build them there than to cut through rocky hills. Of course, the canal would have to be higher than the river; sometimes much higher. Often it was like a notch or shelf cut into the hillside above the river, and held up on the side next to the river by banks of earth which were sometimes high and steep.

In Ohio, two long canals were built. One of these ran from Toledo, on Lake Erie, to Cincinnati, on the Ohio River; the other, from Cleveland, on Lake Erie, to Portsmouth, on the Ohio River. There were some shorter canals connecting with these.

Indiana built a long canal running from Lake Erie through the cities of Fort Wayne and Terre Haute down to Evansville, on the Ohio River. In Illinois, they built the canal which a French explorer, Louis Joliet, had first thought of, a hundred and fifty years before, from Lake Michigan to the Illinois River.

The Steersman

Chapter V

WHAT ARE CANAL BOATS LIKE?

THE first canal boats were intended mostly for the hauling of freight, though they did carry a few passengers. A little later "packet boats" were built, which carried nothing but passengers.

The canal boats were clumsy-looking things. Those which carried freight were like our barges nowadays. At the front end they were a little rounded, so that they would not be too hard to pull through the water.

They never had sharp, slender prows, for that would have been a waste of space in the hull. The boatmen needed all the space in the boats that they could get.

The boats were pulled by horses or mules. These walked along a broad path called the towpath, at the edge of the water. They were attached to the boat by a rope, called the tow-rope, which was at least two hundred feet long, and sometimes two hundred and fifty feet. They were hitched in tandem style—that is, they walked one behind the other; and one of the boat's crew—very often a boy—walked behind them with a whip, to see that they kept moving.

Two or three horses were used to pull the largest and heaviest boats. It seems remarkable that two horses could draw a boat containing a hundred tons or more of cargo, in addition to the weight of the boat itself, but this is true. They had to strain and pull hard for a moment or two until they got the boat moving, but after it was started, they worked no harder than if they were pulling a loaded wagon. Now and then one would see a smaller boat pulled by only one horse.

We have been calling them horses all the time, but there were far more mules than horses working on the canals. The canal men said that mules lived longer and could pull more weight than a horse.

Each boat had a captain. The captain might also be the owner of the boat. Then there was a crew to do the work. There might be only one man in the crew beside the captain, but on the larger and busier freight boats there might be as many as five. One of

WHAT ARE CANAL BOATS LIKE? 27

these was the steersman and another the driver. The others were deck hands, who helped load or unload cargo and did various other chores. The steersman stood at the stern of the boat and kept it in the middle of the canal by means of the rudder, which he moved by a long handle.

Captains often employed boys as drivers, because they did not have to pay boys as high wages as they did men. James A. Garfield, who became President of the United States, was a driver for a boat on the canals in Ohio when he was only sixteen years old.

On the larger boats, there was also a cook—for the crew lived on the boat. They ate their meals and slept in very small rooms built in either the bow or the stern. The cook was sometimes a man, sometimes a woman.

On some canals the boats did not run at night. Late in the evening they would tie up to the bank, starting again next morning at dawn. On busy canals such as the Erie, many boats kept going during the night, just as railroad trains do. On such boats, there were two drivers, two steersmen, and two cooks, so that one group could work while the other slept. Canal boatmen worked twelve or more hours a day, and made no complaint about it.

Canal-Boat Mule

An Old English Lock

Chapter VI
THE LOCKS

WHY do we say "upstream" and "downstream" about a canal? Because the water in the canals does not stand still. Canals are built so that there is a very, very slow current. It is so slow that if you drop a stick into the water you can scarcely tell which way it is moving. In most canals the water does not move as much as a quarter of a mile in an hour. The current must not be strong, else the horses can not pull loaded boats against it. Yet there must be a little current, in order to make the locks work properly.

What is a lock? It is the device by which a canal is able to go down a steep hill into a valley without having any waterfalls or any swift current in it. No one knows who invented the lock, although some have thought that it was invented in Italy a little more than four centuries ago. We now find that the Chinese were using locks on their Grand Canal five hundred years ago, and it may be that they were the first who thought of this clever piece of machinery.

Perhaps some of us have seen a canal lock. It is an enclosure through which the canal flows. Nowadays it is built of concrete; but on our early canals, its side-walls were usually of brick or stone. The space in the lock was just a little larger than the largest boats. The lock is closed at each end by a pair of heavy gates, which on our old canals, were made of wood. These gates are like double doors, turning on hinges and meeting in the middle of the passage. When they are closed, they stop the water from flowing.

One of these pairs of gates, usually the upper pair—that is, at the end of the lock which was upstream—must always be kept closed; for the surface of the water in the canal above the lock might be six or eight or ten feet feet higher than the surface of the water below the lock.

Let us suppose that a boat is going upstream. The lower gates of the lock are open, and the boat is pulled into the lock. Then the lower gates are closed and the upper gates are partly opened, so that water flows into the lock—but not too fast—and fills it. As the water rises, the boat rises with it. Within two or three minutes, the water inside the lock is on a level with the water in the canal on the upstream side of the lock. The upper gates are now opened wide, the boat passes into the canal and goes on upstream.

But suppose the boat is going downstream. It stops near the lock. The lower lock gates are closed, and the upper ones partly opened. Water quickly fills the lock, and the boat passes into it. The upper gates are then closed again and little shutters in the lower gates are opened. The water now passes slowly out, and the boat is seen going down until it is on a level with the water below the lock. Then the lower gates are opened, and the boat passes out.

When the horses pull the boat into the lock, the steersman has to pilot it very carefully, especially if it happens to be one of the biggest boats; for sometimes the space in the lock is only a few inches wider than the boat.

The man who opened and closed the lock gates was called the lock-tender. He always lived in a house close by, and on some of the more busy canals, he had

A Lock

a hard job. Usually he had a garden in which he raised his own vegetables; he would have fruit trees, a cow, some hogs and chickens. Thus he and his family produced nearly all of their own food, and he had to buy from the store only a few such things as flour, salt, sugar, and coffee.

On most of the canals each boat carried a horn or a conch-shell on which the captain or the steersman would blow long blasts as they came near a lock. The lock-tender might be hoeing his potatoes or feeding his hogs when the boat came along, and it was necessary to warn him. Sometimes when he was too busy, his wife or one of his children would go out and move the gates.

On the earliest canals, the lock gates had long poles or levers attached to them, by which they were opend and closed; but before many canals had been built in America, a windlass was invented which worked much better. The lock-tender just turned a crank, and long chains ran from the windlass to the gates, to pull them open or shut.

In hilly country, where there were many locks, canal travel was very slow. The Chemung Canal, which ran from Seneca Lake to Elmira, New York, was twenty-three miles long and had forty-nine locks on it—more than two locks in every mile. To travel on that canal was just going through one lock after another. There were other short canals which were almost as bad.

On a few canals there were so many boats and the

THE LOCKS

business was so heavy that the lock-tender did not have much time to cultivate a garden. He often had to work at the lock from twelve to sixteen hours a day.

Approaching a Lock at Night

On these busy canals there were nearly always traffic jams at the locks. There might be dozens of boats above and below, each waiting for its turn to pass through. Sometimes the jam would extend for a mile or more in each direction.

On the canals where the boats did not run all night, there were always many boats tied up overnight near the locks, waiting to get through. The lock-tender must begin work at dawn—which, in midsummer, was before four o'clock in the morning—to put the boats through the lock as fast as possible. At seven o'clock he stopped for an hour to eat his breakfast, and boats had to wait. At eight o'clock he began again, and worked until noon. Then he took an hour off for what we call lunch nowadays, but which they called dinner then. Then he worked again until six o'clock in the evening, at which time he took another hour off to eat his supper. At seven o'clock he began "locking" boats through again, and kept it up until nine or ten that night. That was an ordinary day's work!

The Erie Canal was very busy and the boats did not stop even at meal times. Every lock-tender had a helper, who worked the locks while the tender was eating his meals. On the Erie and other canals where the boats ran all night, there were two sets of lock-tenders, one for daytime, and the other for night.

Blowing the Conch-Shell

Chapter VII

THE CANAL AND THE FARMERS

WHEN the canals were first dug, many farmers who lived near them built their own boats to carry their produce to market. Merchants and traders also had their own boats, in which they shipped cattle, furs, salt, and other freight. Many of these boats were made by men who had never done any boat-building before. The job was very poorly done. Some of the boats leaned to one side when they were put into the water; some were heavier at one end than at the other; some were very hard to steer. But the worst trouble with most of them was that their hulls leaked so badly that the cargo got wet, and some of the boats would sink every few miles.

When a boat sank, it did not go out of sight, because the water was hardly ever more than four or five feet deep. But when a boat sank, its cargo was likely to be ruined by the wetting. Other boatmen became very angry, too, when they came along and found a boat sunken, partly or wholly blocking the channel. Sometimes it took a day or two to get the water pumped out of a sunken boat, the leaky seams patched, and the boat raised again.

After the first year or two along a new canal, men learned how to build better boats, and the farmers were more likely to let the regular boatmen carry their produce.

When a farmer loaded his own boat and started for a town such as Utica or Harrisburg to sell his grain or hogs, he sometimes had one or two of his sons in his crew, or perhaps the hired man who worked on his farm, or one or two of his neighbors. If it was the first trip, probably none of these men had ever been very far from home before, and knew but little about the country through which they were passing. They would go along, asking other boatmen, "How far is it to Utica?" At night they would tie the boat to the bank, often just where it would be in the way of other boats, and they would go to sleep. At daybreak next morning one of them would cook breakfast, they would eat, and start on their way again.

A funny story is told of one of these boats. A farmer started for Harrisburg with his crop on his boat, going down the Pennsylvania Canal, which ran along the Susquehanna River. One night, after a hard day's work, his crew tied the boat to the bank, not far from a regular freight boat. They were very tired and slept soundly. During the night, the men on the freight boat slyly loosened the farmer's boat from the bank and turned it around, heading it upstream. The farmer and his crew did not waken.

Next morning, not noticing the change in their di-

THE CANAL AND THE FARMERS 37

rection, they hitched up their horses and started right back over the canal through which they had passed the day before. After going several miles, they came to a small town. One of the men, looking about him in surprise, said, "Why, this looks just like a town we came through yesterday." Not until then did they learn of the joke that had been played on them.

Packet Boat on a Pennsylvania Canal

Chapter VIII
WHAT THE BOATS CARRIED

Look at the boats coming from the farming country, going towards the cities on any of the canals. Down in Virginia they are creeping on towards Richmond. On the Chesapeake and Ohio Canal they are headed towards Washington. On the canals in Pennsylvania they are bound for Pittsburgh, Harrisburg or Philadelphia; and on the New England canals, for Boston, Providence, New Haven, or Worcester. On the Erie Canal they move towards Buffalo, Rochester, Syracuse, Oswego, Albany, and New York. On the middle western canals, they are going towards Cleveland, Toledo, Columbus, Cincinnati, Fort Wayne, Chicago.

These boats are loaded with the merchandise—most of it something to eat—which the farmers and workers in the small towns and villages have produced. Here is a barge full of wheat. Yonder comes another loaded with corn. Just behind it is one full of potatoes and apples and onions. Others carry oats or rye. On yet others you find barrels of cider, barrels of vinegar, molasses, salt pork, or flour, bags of corn meal, crates of eggs. On another you will see hams and

WHAT THE BOATS CARRIED

bacon; for these meats were not then made ready to eat in big factories, as they are now; in those days, they were smoked in little smoke-houses out on the farms.

Here comes a boat from which a strong odor blows out as it passes us. The captain tells us that it is laden with furs. The furs come from trappers—some of them white men, some Indians—who catch the animals far back in the deep forests surrounding the Great Lakes.

Another boat is nearly full of bags of wool, clipped from sheep which graze on the prairies of Indiana and Illinois. We see large rolls of leather, too, tanned by men who own little village tanneries. Some of them do most of the work themselves, and may not have more than one or two employes. One of these rolls of leather is very important to such a man, and he is very anxious about it until he hears that it has been delivered, and he receives his pay for it.

Listen to the squealing and grunting which come from that big boat over there! It is full of live hogs, going to the city, where the butchers will soon turn them into pork chops, roasts and sausage. A plaintive mooing in another boat tells us that it is loaded with cattle, which the city people will soon be eating in the form of steaks, roasts, meat pies and hash.

And here in this boat—what an uproar of cackling and squawking and crowing is heard inside it! Its cargo cannot be anything else than live chickens on their way to market. Its boatmen look unhappy. It is no fun, riding for several days with a boat-load of chickens. One day, in 1825, an Erie Canal boat passed Albany with a thousand turkeys, ducks and geese on board. Just fancy the noise! These fowls were being sent to the West Indies.

From Syracuse, where there were great salt factories, you saw whole boat-loads of salt going this way and that. Rochester had several large flour mills, and many boat-loads of wheat came into that town, with many loads of flour going out. From cities like Boston, New York and Philadelphia came boats loaded with manufactured goods and things from foreign countries—machinery, tools, farm implements, hardware, sewing machines, sugar, coffee, dried fish, and many other kinds of freight.

Men who owned a stone quarry, a gravel pit, or a fine bank of sand close to a canal were fortunate, for those things could be sold readily in the days when towns were growing fast and many new buildings were being erected. Canal boats carried many tons of these things. Brick, lime, cement, lumber, and other things used in building houses were also carried in large quantities.

Now and then you might see some queer cargoes; boats, for example, loaded with nothing but ashes! Why were ashes being saved? Because they were used in making lye and soap—the strong, yellow-brown soap that was used in those days for washing clothes. Before coal was discovered, everybody burned

WHAT THE BOATS CARRIED

wood. It was used not only to warm homes, but to supply the fire for locomotives and steamboat boilers, in factories and potteries—wherever heat was needed. So thousands of boat-loads of wood were carried to the towns and cities. Poor people with baskets in their hands went about the docks where the wood was unloaded, picking up bits of bark and small sticks for their own home fires.

After anthracite coal became well known, most of the boats on the Delaware and Hudson Canal, the canals of eastern Pennsylvania and the two canals which crossed New Jersey from the Delaware River to New York harbor were busy hauling coal. But in the upper part of New York State, in New England, in Virginia, and in the middle west, wood was still the fuel which everybody used, and it still filled many canal boats.

There were even long, slender rafts of logs, fastened together by ropes and chains and towed through the canals. Men stood a few yards apart on the logs, with poles in their hands, to keep the raft away from the bank. These rafts were considered a great nuisance by boatmen, because they got in the way of boats.

A Raft, with Guiding "Sweeps"

Chapter IX

HOW THE CANALS HELPED BUSINESS

A GREAT deal of the freight carried on the Erie Canal was going to or from New York City. From Albany, where the canal ended, the route was down the Hudson River to New York. Boats which came through the canal fully loaded with freight for New York, did not unload it at Albany, but were towed down the Hudson to New York by steamboat or tug.

Here at Albany is a boat-load of flour from Rochester; another of salt and soda from Syracuse; another loaded with pork and potatoes and onions from some small town along the canal; another of live poultry, and all bound for New York. These four barges are tied together by ropes, making what is called a fleet, and a steam tug tows them down the Hudson.

When the boats are unloaded at New York, the captain or the owner of each boat tries to get a load of merchandise to take back. When he finds it, if it is going all the way to Buffalo, at the other end of the canal, so much the better. But if times are dull, and the boat has waited several days without finding a cargo, it may have to be towed back to Albany

CANALS HELPED BUSINESS

empty. Then the owner will not earn much money on the trip.

When canals were first built in Ohio, Indiana and Illinois, where there were no large towns at that time, the farmers, the traders, the trappers, and the owners of little country flour and corn mills sent their produce all the way to Buffalo or Albany or New York by water. From Ohio or Indiana it travelled by canal to Cleveland or Toledo, on Lake Erie. There it was loaded on steamships or sailing vessels, and taken to Buffalo.

Freight from northern Illinois, going to the cities on the Atlantic coast, travelled by the Illinois and Michigan Canal to Chicago, where it was reloaded into ships. It then went all that long way around through Lake Michigan, Lake Huron, and Lake Erie to reach the Erie Canal at Buffalo.

Farmers in those middlewestern states sometimes hauled their grain fifty miles to reach a canal. The people in those states who had goods to sell had no good market for what they produced before the canals were built. Their profits were therefore very small. With the canals in operation, they began to earn much more. They could sell flour for three times as much in New York as they could get for it in the towns near their homes, and find a market for many things which otherwise they could not have sold at all.

Chapter X

WISE MULES

HORSES and mules did not work steadily all day long. If they had they would soon have been worn out. So they were unhitched from the boat every little while, and given a rest, with something to eat and a drink of water. When they were unfastened from the tow-line, another team of horses was hitched to it, and the boat went on its way. Teams could be changed in a minute, if the captain was in a hurry.

The boats which were owned by their own captains sometimes had their own horses and carried them on the boats when they were not working. Stalls for the horses were built in one end of the boat. Each team worked six hours; then it rested aboard the boat while the other team pulled for six hours. If the boat ran all night, each team would thus work twelve hours a day.

When boats on the Erie Canal had full cargoes for the city of New York, they were taken down the Hudson from Albany by steam tugs. When this happened, the horses would have a long, long rest. It might take a week or two to make the round trip, especially if the boat was held in New York while waiting for a cargo. When you passed one of these boats on the Hudson and saw the horses munching hay, looking contentedly out of the windows of their stalls as the boat glided down the big river, you wondered whether they knew how much luckier they were than horses which had to work every day.

Some other horses had a pretty busy life. There were public horse-stations, ten, twelve, or fifteen miles apart on the larger canals. These were great stables full of mules and horses, owned by men whose business it was to rent animals to canal boats. When a boat came to one of these stations and wanted a fresh team, there was always one ready. The team which had brought the boat would be unhitched, given a rest and a feed and sent back, towing another boat, a few hours later.

Then there were large companies which owned many boats on the canal, and some of these companies had their own horse stations.

The way in which canal boats going in opposite directions passed each other was interesting. There was a towpath on only one side of the canal, and the horses had to walk on the same path going in either direction.

When the two boats met, the boat going upstream had what is called the right of way. That was because it was a little harder to draw a boat against the current than to go downstream. So the team going downstream would walk to the outer side of the towpath—that is, the side farthest from the canal—and stop. The steersman on the downstream boat would steer his boat over to the side of the canal farthest from the towpath. With the team standing still, the tow-line would sink to the bottom of the canal.

The team and boat going upstream would come right along, passing between the downstream boat and its team. The upstream horses, walking close to the edge of the water, would carefully step over the other's tow-line where it lay across the path; and their boat would pass over the part which lay in the water. This done, the downstream team would start again, their bells jingling musically; for nearly every canal boat team had at least one bell tied to a horse's neck, and sometimes more.

A smart team, with long experience on the canal, did not have to be told what to do when it met another boat—especially if it happened to be a team of mules. Many canal boatmen believed that mules were much more intelligent than horses. There is no doubt that a mule will learn to do a regular task more quickly and more accurately than a horse. A good team of canal mules knew when it was going downstream; and when it saw an upstream boat coming near, stepped to the outer side of the towpath and stopped without being told to do so by the driver. The other team knew equally well that it must keep going, and walk on the inner side of the towpath, close to the water.

Chapter XI
LOW BRIDGE

EVEN though the boat did not run all night, the day's work of the canal boatman did not stop at nightfall. The crew always lighted their headlight and lanterns, and pushed on for another two or three hours before they stopped and went to bed.

The headlight that they used was a big, square lamp set near the prow of the boat, with a wooden reflector behind it. Of course they had no electricity in those days, and this lamp was very much like the old kerosene oil lamps which some of us have seen. We did not have any oil wells in this country until about the year 1860. After that time, boatmen began burning kerosene oil in their headlights and lanterns. Before that, they burned either camphene, which is a sort of turpentine, or oil made from the fat of whales.

Canal boats did not often stop when storms came on; they just pushed right ahead. It was not pleasant

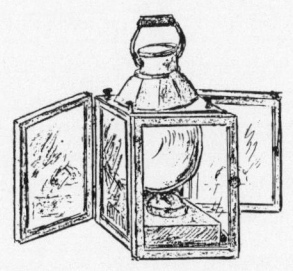

Canal-Boat Headlight

for the driver and steersman when heavy rain was falling, wind blowing, and lightning flashing. Sometimes the wind and rain became really blinding. If the horses were facing it, they would stop without asking leave, and turn their tails towards the storm. They knew when they had enough. This did not often happen, for both horses and boatmen were used to bad weather. The boats did not run in winter, but early in the spring and late in the autumn there were some very cold winds—perhaps even snow—which made it very uncomfortable for the driver, and for the boatmen who had to be outside for hours at a time.

A storm at night was still worse. Sometimes a horse would stumble in the darkness and fall into the canal, dragging the other horses after him. Then there would be shouts of alarm from the driver and steersman. Some of the crew would leap to the bank, while others would plunge into the water, to help get the horses on their feet. If the horses happened to get tangled in the harness when they fell they might drown before they could be rescued. If the driver was a small boy, he often rode one of the horses instead of walking behind the team. When the horses fell, he was likely to go into the canal, too, and be in some danger, although canal boys could usually swim almost as well as ducks.

In level country, the people who built bridges for wagon roads across the canals often did not take the

LOW BRIDGE 49

"Low Bridge, Everybody Down!"

trouble to build them high enough above the water. There were many bridges so low that a man standing upon the deck of a boat could not pass under them; he had to stoop or crouch low to keep from being struck by the bridge. Indeed, some bridges were so low that men on the larger boats either had to go down into the hull or lie flat on the deck to pass under them.

Of course, men who had worked a long time on the canal knew where all the bridges were, and knew whether they were high or low. But if there was a new man who was not familiar with the canal, the steersman watched very carefully and called out "Low bridge!" at the right moment. Even the experienced men on the boats sometimes grew careless and forgot to watch until the steersman drew their attention by crying out, "Low bridge!"

Danger from bridges was especially great at night, and the steersman had to be very watchful, straining his eyes through the darkness, for it might be a very serious thing to be struck by a bridge.

Canal workers had hardships which we now find it hard to picture. But after all, they had a great deal of fun. On a fair day, if there were not too many locks to go through and no cargo to be loaded or unloaded, it was very pleasant to sit or lie on the deck of the boat and glide along with little to do, greeting friends on shore or on other boats, joking, telling stories and singing songs. The men had songs all their own. The most famous was one about the Erie Canal. These were some of its words:—

1. I've got a mule, her name is Sal,
   Fifteen miles on the Erie Canal.
   She's a good old worker and a good old pal,
   Fifteen miles on the Erie Canal.

   We've hauled some barges in our day,
   Filled with lumber, coal and hay,
   And we know ev'ry inch of the way
   From Albany to Buffalo.

   Chorus:
   Low bridge, everybody down!
   Low bridge, for we're going through a town;
   And you'll always know your neighbor,
   You'll always know your pal,
   If you ever navigated on the Erie Canal.

Gossip

Chapter XII

LIFE ON THE CANAL

EVERY canal boat had a name, and no two boats on a canal were permitted to have the same one. We may be sure that every canal had one boat named in honor of George Washington; and nearly all had boats named *Andrew Jackson* and *Daniel Webster*.

Boats owned by their captains often had the name of the captain's wife or some other member of his family. Now and then you saw a boat that was named for two people—such as *Hattie and Mattie, Cynthia and Sarah*, or *John and Annie*. There were others with such names as *Two Sisters, Four Brothers, Three Partners* and so on.

There were boats named for animals and birds, and even for some of the insects. You would not be surprised to see boats named *Lion, Tiger, Eagle, Bluebird* and *Dolphin*, or even *Elephant* and *Whale*; but who would expect to find boats named *Rat, Fly* or *Flea*? Yet there really were such names.

Each captain painted his boat according to his own taste. A basin full of boats would therefore show all the colors of the rainbow.

Canals in the northern part of the country did not operate during the winter. As soon as the weather became cold enough to freeze ice on the water, the boats had to stop running; for the horses could not pull the boats if there was even a thin sheet of ice.

On most canals, the winter months were spent in making repairs. As soon as the boats ceased running, the water was shut off in the feeders, and the canal was drained. Then, when the channel was dry, the lock gates could be repaired and the aqueducts patched where they had begun to leak. Wherever earth or sand had been washed into the channel by heavy rains the channel would be cleaned out and made deep again. Cracks and weak spots in the banks were repaired and made strong.

When spring came, and there seemed to be no more danger of hard freezing, the water would be turned

LIFE ON THE CANAL

into the channel and you would read in the newspapers that the canal was open for business, and boats were moving once more.

The Erie Canal was usually closed from about the first of December to the first of April—four months. Sometimes it stayed open a little longer, but there were long, cold winters when it had to be closed for five months. Farther south, you found that the canals did not have to shut down for nearly so long. The Chesapeake and Ohio Canal, which ran along the Potomac River, and the canals in Southern Ohio, were often closed for not more than a month. There were winters during which the canal along the James River, in Virginia, did not have any ice on it at all.

Of course there was never any ice on the Santee Canal, in South Carolina. Things were so different there that the managers would close the canal for cleaning and repairs in July and August, which were the months when business was dull.

When a large number of boats were crowded together in a basin to spend the winter, they became a sort of village. There would be several captains who had their families with them on their boats. With their boats moored side by side, Captain A's wife would step right over to Mrs. B's boat for a call, so that they all became almost like one big family. The children went to school in the town near by; they played together on deck or went coasting and snowballing on shore. Meanwhile, the men would be making repairs on the boats, and getting other kinds of work to do if they could.

At last the cold winds of March would die away; the air would grow milder; only little patches of snow would be left in the shade on the hillsides. A robin would be heard singing one morning; buds on the trees would begin to swell, and little green plants would break through the moist earth. Then the news would come, "They are turning the water into the canal. It will be open next Monday." This was welcome news, indeed, for now the men would begin earning money again.

On Monday there would be a great bustle. Men now shouted back and forth as they untied ropes and pushed the boats with poles, getting them out of the basin and into the canal again. Women and children called out, "Goodbye!" to each other. The horses were hitched to the tow-lines and plodded away, the boats trailing slowly after. The year's work had begun.

Canal-Boat Neighbors

Chapter XIII

THE PASSENGER BOATS

THE packet boats, built for passengers only, were usually larger than the freight boats. They also had sharper prows, so that they could be moved faster. Each packet had at least three horses and sometimes four. The owners took much pride in their boats, and claimed that they were very fine and comfortable. They were pleasant enough to ride on in the daytime, if the boat was not too crowded. But at night, there was far less comfort.

There were large companies on each canal which owned lines of packet boats. Runners or solicitors from each of these companies would meet every traveler who stepped from a stagecoach in the large towns along the canal. Each runner would try to persuade the traveler to buy a ticket by his line, loudly declaring that it had the finest, fastest and most comfortable boats, and served the best meals.

The packet boats had time-tables; they left each town on the canal at regular hours each day, just as railroad trains do. Perhaps it would be more correct to say that they tried to leave at regular times each day, for they were very often late. There were many things to hinder them—storms driving against the boat, heavy traffic on the canal, and traffic jams at the locks. A traveler over the Erie Canal in early days tells of having to wait two hours to get through a lock at Utica.

It was a law on the canals that whenever a packet came up behind a freight boat going in the same direction, the freight boast must let the packet pass. The freight team stopped, and the packet passed between the freight boat and its team, in much the same way that two boats passed each other when they were going in opposite directions.

In the bow or front part of the packet boat there was a small room where the crew slept. Next came another small sleeping room, this one for the women passengers; and next, in the middle of the boat, was the main cabin, the largest room on the vessel. This was the dining room and parlor during the day, and at night the men slept in it. The sleeping space for the women and girls was much smaller than the men's because there were fewer women travelling than men. In the stern of the boat were the pantry and kitchen, where the food for the passengers and crew was cooked.

These cabins would seem very small to us now. The ceiling was not much higher than the head of a tall man. The passengers did not usually sit inside the boat unless the weather was cool, or unless it was raining or very windy outside. In cool weather the main cabin would be warmed by a tiny stove which burned wood.

THE PASSENGER BOATS 57

In fair weather, it was more pleasant to sit on deck—that is, on the roof of the boat—talking and looking at the scenery as the boat glided along. Some of the ladies had their knitting and crochet work; some were reading. If the sun was very hot, some people raised their umbrellas. Canal travel was pleasant, indeed, at such times. The movement of the boat was smooth and steady. There were no bumps or jerks such as we have on railroad trains and buses. There was no smoke, no smell of gasoline, no noise of machinery.

Now and then some of the passengers would step ashore when the boat was in a lock, and enjoy a walk on the towpath. There were places where the canal was so crooked and curving that a walker could take a short cut across the curve, linger to gather wild strawberries, and still keep up with the boat.

If it was raining, or if the weather was cold, the passengers had to sit inside the cabin. There some talked, others read books or newspapers, ladies did their fancy work, and a group would sometimes gather around the little organ or piano which the packets usually carried, and sing.

For Cool Days on Board

Chapter XIV

BEFORE PULLMAN'S DAY

THE fare for passengers on the best packets was five cents a mile; and the boat supplied meals and berths for sleeping while you were aboard, without extra charge.

The sleeping arrangements were very queer. There were no separate berths with curtains in front of them, so that you could be private, as you are in a railroad sleeping car. During the day, you saw nothing which looked like a bed—though you might have noticed three or four rows of small holes in the walls, running all the way around the cabin.

But about nine o'clock in the evening, the crew would begin bringing the berths out of a storage closet and putting them in place. They were just like narrow cots, consisting of a piece of canvas stretched on a frame of iron rods. The rods at the head and the foot extended a few inches beyond the frame. The ends of these rods on one side were thrust into the holes in the wall, while on the outer side the cots were supported by strong ropes hanging from the ceiling. In each berth was a very thin pad stuffed with straw. This was called the mattress. There were at least three tiers of berths and sometimes four, one above another, all around the cabin.

We are told that the berths on most boats were less than two feet wide. Of course you had to be very careful when turning over in such a bed. Fat passengers, if they could not get a lower berth, often preferred to sleep on the floor. Some very heavy people could not squeeze themselves into the berths at all.

It often happened that there were more passengers than there were berths. At such times, one or two men would sleep—or try to sleep—on the dining table, while others lay on the floor.

Small ropes were stretched across the cabin while the passengers were going to bed, and on these the passengers hung their clothing. This was such a bother and the space was so small that most men took off only a part of their clothes. The same scenes took place in the women's cabin as in the men's, where, since their room was smaller, they were likely to be even more crowded.

In every cabin full of passengers, there was sure to be some one who snored. He was always regarded by his fellow-travelers as a dreadful nuisance. The traveler who had to get off the boat at some town which was reached in the middle of the night also caused many unkind remarks as he stumbled and bumped around the dimly-lighted cabin, searching for his baggage. Now and then he would get entangled with the clothes-line or step on some sleeper who lay on the floor.

At six o'clock in the morning one of the crew would go around shaking all the men until they were awake, and telling them to get up, so that the berths could be put away and the room be made ready for serving breakfast.

These packet boats were always neatly painted; usually white outside, with red or green window casings. Their names were intended to show how fast or how fine they were. Such names as *Racer, Lightning, Swiftsure, Express, Whirlwind, Meteor* or *Greyhound* were given to boats that could not move more than four or five miles an hour. People who had traveled on a packet boat and endured its inconveniences, sometimes wondered why it was named *Splendid* or *Fashion* or *Palace*.

The packet horses were finer than those of the freight boats, and did not have to work so long at a time. On the main Pennsylvania Canal running between Pittsburgh and Johnstown, a distance of one hundred and three miles, the packets used thirteen teams. Each team pulled the boat a little less than eight miles. The packet *Silver Bell*, on the Wabash and Erie Canal, in Indiana, was always drawn by three gray horses, with silver-mounted harness and silver bells jingling at their throats.

The mail was carried for many years on canal packet boats.

Chapter XV

LINE BOATS AND HOUSE BOATS

THE real packet boats did not carry any freight at all. But there were some second-class boats called *line boats* which carried both passengers and freight. They were not as comfortable to ride on as the packets, and the food served on their tables was not as good. But while the packets charged five cents a mile for passage, the line boats carried passengers for a cent and a half a mile. They charged extra for meals; or the passenger could take his own food with him if he liked.

The line boats were much slower than the packets. Their horses were slower, they did not have a special right of way over other boats, as the packets did, and they were often delayed while loading and unloading freight. They seldom travelled more than forty miles a day, even if they ran all night; while the packets could cover as much as eighty or ninety miles a day.

Persons who were moving from one town to another, or from one part of the country to another, and who hadn't much money, often used the line boats. These people could ship their household goods, spinning wheels, plows, and even, if necessary, the family cow and horse, on the boat on which they themselves were traveling.

The canals had much to do with increasing the population of the states lying west of Pennsylvania, in the Ohio and Mississippi Valleys and around the Great Lakes. At the time when the canals were at their best—that is, between 1825 and 1850—thousands of people from the New England states, from New York, New Jersey, eastern Pennsylvania, and even from Maryland and Delaware, moved westward on the line boats every year. They were seeking new homes in the Middle West, where farming land was fertile and still very low in price, and where new towns were springing up, giving fine opportunities for merchants, artisans, attorneys, and doctors.

Thousands of immigrants were coming to America every year, too. Most of them in those days came from England, Ireland and Germany. Large numbers of them went to the Middle Western States, and nearly all of them travelled in line boats on the canals. Many times a day the people living near the canal saw boats move slowly by, their decks covered with these new citizens from beyond the sea, sitting patiently among their bundles of clothing and bedding.

There are many of our people now, living in the Middle West and elsewhere in America, whose ancestors moved westward on canal boats in those early days.

Some families in the East who wished to move far-

LINE BOATS AND HOUSE BOATS

ther west built their own little house boats and lived in them while they were being towed through the canals. Such a boat could start at New York, for example, and be towed through the Delaware and Raritan Canal and the Delaware River to Philadelphia. From Philadelphia it could go by the Pennsylvania Canal to Pittsburgh. From there it might go by canal out into Ohio, or it could float down the Ohio River with the current, and might stop wherever the family chose, along the shores of Ohio, Indiana, Illinois or Kentucky. There a new home would be founded and the man would either start farming, go into business, or seek employment as a workman.

Packet Boat Crossing on Aqueduct

Chapter XVI

WHAT HAVE THE CANALS DONE FOR US?

THE United States was a young nation when the canals were first built. They made it grow and prosper.

All classes of people were helped by the canals. Farmers could send their crops to better markets more cheaply than before. Merchants and manufacturers were able to send their goods easily to towns which could not be reached before, and the rates which the boats charged for carrying the goods were low. The cost of doing business was less, and there was more employment for workingmen.

New towns were founded and became cities because they were on the course of some important canal. Buffalo, Rochester, Utica and Syracuse, all in the state of New York, are large cities today just because they were on the Erie Canal, and were thus given a good start. Cleveland, Toledo and Cincinnati in Ohio, Fort Wayne in Indiana and other cities were also aided by the canals that ran to them or through them when they were but villages or small towns.

But these inland canals had only just begun to prosper when the steam locomotive was invented. That

A Tug-Boat Towing a Fleet of Canal Boats Down the Hudson River

hurt their business. When railroads were built, people wanted to travel faster, and to ship their goods more quickly than they could by canal. The canals, for many years, still continued to do business, for goods can always be sent more cheaply by water. But the packet boats soon disappeared, and only such things as coal, sand, stone, brick, and other low-grade freight was carried on the canals.

One after another these old waterways had to give up. Every now and then a canal would be flooded and its banks torn out, and the managers would decide that they could not afford to repair it again. So that canal would pass out of existence.

There were four thousand four hundred miles of canals built in the United States in the early years of its history, and only about four hundred miles of those same canals are in use now. Some of the canals have been so completely destroyed that you cannot always find the place where their channels used to run.

The Erie Canal was the greatest success of them all. While other canals were being abandoned, it continued to prosper. In 1870 there were nearly seven thousand boats running on it; so many that the canal was just one big traffic jam. At almost any time in the day you could stand on a bridge across this canal and see a continuous line of boats, following each other closely, stretching away in both directions as far as the eye could reach. At nights their headlights looked as if a great torchlight procession was going by.

WHAT HAVE CANALS DONE? 67

That crowding and slow movement of boats was a bad thing for the canal. The locks were doubled, so that boats could pass through them in both directions at once; the channel was made wider and deeper. Still it was too small. The railroads which ran alongside it carried freight much faster, and operated the whole year around. The canal must be closed for several months in the winter. In 1900 there were still two thousand boats on the canal, but its business was steadily growing smaller. Meanwhile it had paid the state of New York many, many millions of dollars in profits; it had made New York the *Empire State*, and it had been one of the greatest builders of the nation.

Soon after 1900 the state of New York began rebuilding it. It was greatly widened, many curves in the old canal were straightened, fine concrete locks with steel gates were built, and the waterway is now called the New York State Barge Canal. Steam tugs and steam canal boats run through it.

The last canal on which horses pulled boats was that one which follows the Lehigh and Delaware Rivers from Mauch Chunk down to Bristol, in Pennsylvania. The great mines at Mauch Chunk sent anthracite coal down that canal until 1931, when the boats ceased to run. After that, all the Lehigh coal was shipped by railroad. Only a few pleasure boats ever use that canal now.

It is sad to come across the ruined walls of an old lock, as we sometimes do, overgrown with vines and

68 WHEN HORSES PULLED BOATS

bushes, and to think of how important it once was, and what busy, pleasant scenes took place there long ago. We should never forget how much the canals aided in making the United States a great nation.

Nor is the usefulness of canals wholly past. Today we hear but little of them as they were in the olden days. What we now hear about is such mammoth waterways as Panama, Suez, and Sault Ste. Marie. Here millions of tons of shipping and freight pass through each year, making a tale of giant forces by the side of which the old towpath waterways were but little children.

Alvin F. Harlow
1936

*The Old Canal Boat Gave Way to
the Steam Locomotive and
Then to the Automobile*

CANAL BIBLIOGRAPHY

Abbott,, Willis J. - "Panama and the Canal" (1913)

American Canal Society - "Best from American Canals" (1980)

American Public Works Association - "History of Public Works in the United States" (1976)

American Society of Civil Engineers - "Biographical Dictionary of American Civil Engineers (1972)

Anness, Milford - "Low Bridge and Locks Ahead" Whitewater Canal (1972)

Baer, Christopher - "Canal and Railroads of the Mid-Atlantic States 1800 - 1860" (1981)

Basset, John M. & Petrie A. R. - "William Hamilton Merritt" (1974)

Bishop, James B. "The Panama Gateway" (1913)

Boucher, Cyril - "James Brindley" (1972)

Brown, Alexander Crosby - "The Dismal Swamp Canal"

Bracegirdle, Brian and Miles, Patricia H. - "Thomas Telford" (1973)

Clarke, Mary Stetson - "The Old Middlesex Canal" (1974)

Condon, George - "Stars in the Water" (1974)

Conservation Dept., State of Illinois - "Illinois & Michigan Canal State Trailway" (1974)

Cummings, Hubertis M. - "Pennsylvania Board of Canals Commission Records" (1959)

Dunaway, Weyland Fuller - "History of the James River and Kanawha Co."

Dunbar, Seymour - "History of Travel in America" (1937)

Fisher, Allan C., Jr. - "American Inland Waterways" (1973)

Fatout, Paul - "Indiana Canals" (1972)

Gallatin, Albert - "Public Roads and Canals" - 1808 (1968 reprint)

Gard, R. Max - "The Sandy and Beaver Canal" (1952)

Gray, Ralph - "The National Waterway" (1967)

Hadfield, Charles - "The Canal Age" (1968)

Hadfield, Charles - "Afloat in America" (1979)

Hahn, Thomas F. - "George Washington's Canal at Great Falls, Va." (1976)

Harlow, Alvin F. - "Old Towpaths" (1926)

Hepburn, A. Barton - "Artificial Waterways of the World" (1909)

Heisler, John P. - "Canals of Canada" (1973)

Holton, Gladys Reid - "The Genessee Valley Canal" (1971)

Howe, Walter A. - "Documentary History of the Illinois and Michigan Canal" (1956)

Hyde, Charles K. - "Upper Penninsula of Michigan" (1978)

Jackson, John N. - "Welland and the Welland Canal" (1975)

Jacobs, David L. & Neville, Anthony E. - "Bridges, Canals & Tunnels" (1968)

Judson, Clara Ingram - "St. Lawrence Seaway" (1959)

Kirkwood, James I. - "Waterway to the West" (1963)

Kulik, Gary - "Rhode Island Inventory of Historic Engineering and Industrial Sites" (1978)

Langbein, W. B. - "Hydrology and Environmental Aspects of the Erie Canal" (1976)

Lee, James - "The Morris Canal" (1974)

Legget, Robert - "The Canals of Canada"

Legget, Robert - "Rideau Waterway" (1972)

LeRoy - "The Delaware and Hudson Canal" (1980)

Lewis, Gene D. - "Charles Ellet, Jr. 1810 - 1862" (1968)

Lewis, M. J. T. - Slatcher, W. N. & Jarvis, P. N. - "Flashlocks on English Waterways" (1969)

Livingood, James W. - "Philadelphia-Baltimore Trade Rivalry" 1780-1860 (1947)

Ludwig, Edward J. III - "The Chesapeake and Delaware Canal" (1979)

Marshall, Logan - "Story of the Panama Canal" (1913)

Mayhill, Dora Thomas - "Old Wabash and Erie Canal in Carroll County" (1953)

McCulloch, David - "The Path Between the Seas" (1977)

McCullough, Robert & Leuba, Walter - "The Pennsylvania Main Line Canal" (1976)

McKelvey, William J., Jr. - "Champlain to Chesapeake" (1978)

McKelvey, William J., Jr. - "The Delaware & Raritan Canal" (1975)

Miller, John P. - "The Lehigh Canal" (1979)

Mitchell & Hinman - "Internal Improvements in the USA - 1835" (1972)

Morton, Eleanor - "Josiah White, Prince of Pioneers" (1946)

Myer, Donald B. - "Building the Potomac Aqueduct" (1975)
O'Donnell, Thomas C. - "Snubbing Posts" (1972)
Payne, Robert - "The Canal Builders" (1959)
Pennsylvania Canal Society - "History of the Monongahela Navigation 1873" (1978 reprint)
Phillips, John - "Inland Navigation, 1792" (1970)
Porcher, F.A. - "The Santee Canal" (1970)
Potterf, Rex M. - "Wabash and Erie Canal" (1970)
Roberts, Christopher - "The Middlesex Canal" (1938)
Ryan, David D. - "Falls of the James" (1975)
Sanderlin, Walter S. - "The Great National Project: A History of the Chesapeake and Ohio Canal" (1946)
Sanderson, Dorothy H. - "Delaware and Hudson Canalway" (1972)
Scheiber, Harry N. - "Ohio Canal Era" (1960)
Shank, William H. - "The Amazing Pennsylvania Canals" (1981)
Shank, William H - "300 Years with the Pennsylvania Traveler" (1976)
Smith, Peter L. - "Canal Barges and Narrow Boats" (1975)
Snyder, Frank E. & Guss, Byron H. - "The District (C.E.)" (1974)
Squires, Roger W. - "Canals Revived" (1979)
Swanson, Leslie C. - "Canals of Mid-America" (1964)
Swetnam, George - "Pennsylvania Transportation" (1968)
Tanner, Henry S. - "Canals and Railroads of USA 1840" (1970 reprint)
Taylor, George Rogers - "The Transportation Revolution 1815-1860" (1951)
Trevorrow, Frank - "Ohio's Canals" (1973)
U. S. Army Engineer Institute for Water Resources - "National Waterways Study - (Maps)"
Veit, Richard F. - "The Old Canals of New Jersey" (1963)
Wakefield, Manville B. - "Coat Boats to Tidewater" (1965)
Western Writers of America - "Water Trails West" (1978)
White, Josiah - "Josiah White's History by Himself" (undated)
Yoder, C. P. - "Delaware Canal Journal" (1972)

Grant's Hill Canal Tunnel in Pittsburgh, Rediscovered in 1967. (Artist-John Johas)

OTHER PUBLICATIONS OF THE AMERICAN CANAL AND TRANSPORTATION CENTER

THE CANALS OF NEW YORK STATE—A publication of the American Canal Society (1991). The canals of the Empire State, past and present, are covered in whole or in part. 8½" x 11" paperback, 48 pages, 85 illustrations.

THE AMAZING PENNSYLVANIA CANALS - 160th Anniversary Edition - By William H. Shank (1991). A much expanded variation of many previous printings. 125 illustrations, and tables of locks and mileages on most of the principal canals in the State, never previously gathered together in one volume. Four-color cover; two-color interior; 128 pages; a definitive work.

TOWPATH GUIDE TO THE CHESAPEAKE AND OHIO CANAL—By Thomas F. Hahn, (1990). A fully illustrated, historical commentary and mile-by-mile directory for the entire 184-mile length of the C. & O. Canal Towpath from Washington, D.C. to Cumberland, Maryland. Excellent maps included. 226 pages.

HISTORIC BRIDGES OF PENNSYLVANIA—By William H. Shank, (1986 Edition). Traces the development of the bridge-building arts from the time of the first covered bridge in America, to modern bridges of the 20th Century. Biographies of such famous bridge builders as John Roebling, Theodore Burr, Charles Ellet and Ralph Modjeski included. Profusely illustrated.

PENNSYLVANIA TRANSPORTATION HISTORY—A Supplement—By William H. Shank (1990). In this book, Mr. Shank has discussed media and devices not covered in his other books. Early river craft, rope ferries, steam boats, inclined planes, gravity railroads, early steam locomotives, horse cars, cable cars, trolley cars, elevated rail and subway systems, and air-travel devices are included. An 8½" x 11" book with 72 pages and approximately 100 old photos, drawings and tables. Four-color cover.

INDIAN TRAILS TO SUPERHIGHWAYS—By William H. Shank, (1988 Edition). History of the development of Pennsylvania's historic roads and the many interesting vehicles used on them. Descriptions of Braddock's Road, Forbes' Road, National Highway, Lancaster Turnpike, Plank Roads, Corduroy Roads, William Penn Highway, Lincoln Highway, Pennsylvania Turnpike and Keystone Shortway. Recent PennDOT plans for completion of Pennsylvania's Interstate Highway System.

THE BEST FROM AMERICAN CANALS—Number 1 (1972-1979). A publication of the American Canal Society, (fourth printing 1988) featuring articles written by canal-buff experts on historic and currently operating canals in the U.S.A., Canada and Europe. An 8½" x 11" paperback, with 88 pages, the book contains 150 illustrations and a world-wide index.

THE BEST FROM AMERICAN CANALS—Number 2 (1980-1983). A publication of the American Canal Society (1990) reprinting articles on historic and currently operating canals in USA and overseas. Featured are the Panama Canal, the Trent-Severn Waterway, and canals in Europe, Thailand and China. 140 illustrations and maps included, and worldwide index. An 8½" x 11" paperback with 88 pages.

THE BEST FROM AMERICAN CANALS—Number 3 (1983-1986). A publication of the American Canal Society (1986), featuring the Canals of New England, metropolitan New York area, Erie Canal, the I. & M. Heritage Corridor, the Tenn-Tom, St. Lawrence Seaway, and Canals of Sweden, Germany and India. 145 illustrations and maps, and a world-wide index. An 8½" x 11" paperback with 88 pages.

THE BEST FROM AMERICAN CANALS—Number 4 (1986-1988). A publication of the American Canal Society (1989), featuring maps of the principal canals of the USA, Erie Canal, Inclined Planes, Morris Canal, S. & T. Canal, Shinnecock Canal, Champlain Canal, Navigation on the Mississippi, Kanawha, Kentucky, Fox, and Muskingum Rivers. 8½" x 11" paperback, 88 pages.

THE BEST FROM AMERICAN CANALS - Number 5 (1989-1991), A publication of the American Canal Society (1991) featuring the Panama Canal History, Florida's Inland Waterways, Middlesex Canal, D. & H. Canal, ACS—CCS Meeting, Pennsylvania Canal Company, Barkley Canal, Chicago River Reversal, "Soo" Locks, Canaller's Diary, Trent-Severn Canal, Rhine-Main-Danube, Barton Swing Aqueduct, Lingqu Canal.

THE BEST FROM AMERICAN CANALS - Number 6 (1991-1993), A publication of the American Canal Society (1993) featuring the Lowell Canals, Champlain Canal, Trans-Jersey Ship Canal, C. & O. Canal, Ohio Canals, Keweenaw Waterway, Arkansas River, Michigan Inland Route, "Mississippi Queen" Trip, Louisiana's B & L Canal, Irish Canals, Main-Danube Canal, Corinth Canal, Japan's Biwa Canal, Montech Waterslope.

HISTORY OF THE YORK-PULLMAN AUTOMOBILE, 1903-1917—By William H. Shank, (1970). History of the "Six-Wheeler" Pullman, and its successors, which almost made York, Pa. the automotive capital of the United States. History of the early automotive industry in Eastern Pennsylvania also included. Profusely illustrated.

TOWPATHS TO TUGBOATS—A History of American Canal Engineering. By Shank, Mayo, Hahn and Hobbs (Fourth Printing, 1992). The works of such famous Canal Engineers as Benjamin Wright, Canvass White, Charles Ellet, William Hamilton Merritt, George Washington Goethals are detailed—with the canals they built. The Erie, the Welland, the "Soo," the Panama, the St. Lawrence Seaway and the Tenn-Tom are among the many waterways described in detail. A 72-page, 8½" x 11" book, the publication contains more than 130 drawings, maps and photographs in USA, Canada and overseas.

GREAT FLOODS OF PENNSYLVANIA - A TWO-HUNDRED YEAR HISTORY - W. H. Shank (Seventh Printing, 1993). Data, photos and non-technical text on all major floods in the Keystone State since records have been kept. Full chapters on the Johnstown Flood and the disastrous floods of 1936, 1955 and 1972 are included. A definitive work.

VANDERBILT'S FOLLY - A HISTORY OF THE PENNSYLVANIA TURNPIKE - W. H. Shank (Ninth Printing, 1989). The railroad war of 1880-85 which created the tunnels and roadbeds for the present turnpike. History of the Turnpike, 1940-1989, included.

THE COLUMBIA-PHILADELPHIA RAILROAD AND ITS SUCCESSOR—William Hasell Wilson, 1896. This book is an on-the-spot account of the building of one of the oldest railroads in America by its chief engineer, later resident engineer for the Pennsylvania Railroad, who purchased it from the Pennsylvania Canal Commissioners. This 1992 reprint is fully illustrated with 45 old photos, maps and drawings. (Second printing).

THE CANALLER'S SONG BOOK - By William Hullfish, Music Instructor, Writer, Singer (Third Edition, 1993). This 88 page, 8-1/2 x 11 book contains forty historic canal ballads (words and music) collected from old records in the northeastern USA over a ten year research period. Illustrated with old canal drawings. Said to be the most comprehensive collection of canal songs ever published.

PICTURE-JOURNEY ALONG THE PENNSYLVANIA MAIN LINE CANAL, 1826 - 1857, By Philip J. Hoffman, P.E. (1993). Edited by William H. Shank, P.E. Full-color drawings of entire state-owned route, Philadelphia to Pittsburgh. 8-1/2" x 11" paperback. 80 pages. Full Hoffman biography included.

Inquiries may be directed to the American Canal and Transportation Center, 809 Rathton Road, York, Pa. 17403. Price list and discount schedule available.